50 Elevated Mac and Cheese Recipes

By: Kelly Johnson

Table of Contents

- Truffle Mac and Cheese
- Lobster Mac and Cheese
- Buffalo Chicken Mac and Cheese
- Bacon and Cheddar Mac and Cheese
- Spinach and Artichoke Mac and Cheese
- Jalapeño Popper Mac and Cheese
- Mac and Cheese with Butternut Squash
- Pesto Mac and Cheese
- Mac and Cheese with Roasted Garlic
- Greek Mac and Cheese with Feta and Spinach
- Smoked Gouda Mac and Cheese
- Mac and Cheese with Caramelized Onions
- Mac and Cheese with Brussels Sprouts
- BBQ Pulled Pork Mac and Cheese
- Mac and Cheese with Blue Cheese and Pear
- Mac and Cheese with Wild Mushrooms
- Mac and Cheese with Sriracha and Lime
- Creamy Tomato Basil Mac and Cheese
- Baked Mac and Cheese with Herb Breadcrumbs
- Mac and Cheese with Crab and Old Bay
- Mac and Cheese with Roasted Red Peppers
- Mac and Cheese with Ground Beef and Chili
- Mac and Cheese with Chicken and Broccoli
- Mac and Cheese with Spicy Italian Sausage
- Mac and Cheese with Goat Cheese and Thyme
- Mac and Cheese with Pumpkin and Sage
- Mac and Cheese with Cauliflower and Cheese Sauce
- Mac and Cheese with Roasted Eggplant
- Mac and Cheese with Zucchini and Herbs
- Mac and Cheese with Boursin and Spinach
- Mac and Cheese with Smoked Salmon
- Mac and Cheese with Sweet Potatoes and Pecans
- Mac and Cheese with Chorizo and Corn
- Mac and Cheese with Pimento Cheese
- Mac and Cheese with Peas and Prosciutto

- Mac and Cheese with Artichokes and Parmesan
- Mac and Cheese with Bacon and Egg
- Mac and Cheese with Truffle Oil and Parmesan
- Mac and Cheese with Cilantro and Lime
- Mac and Cheese with Roasted Veggies
- Mac and Cheese with Italian Herbs and Cheese
- Mac and Cheese with Curry and Coconut Milk
- Mac and Cheese with Aged Cheddar and Mustard
- Mac and Cheese with Broccoli Rabe and Sausage
- Mac and Cheese with Fig and Prosciutto
- Mac and Cheese with Peppers and Onions
- Mac and Cheese with Chicken Alfredo
- Mac and Cheese with Pesto and Sundried Tomatoes
- Mac and Cheese with Fontina and Truffle Salt
- Mac and Cheese with a Mexican Twist (Chiles and Queso)

Truffle Mac and Cheese

Ingredients:

- 8 oz elbow macaroni
- 2 tablespoons butter
- 2 tablespoons all-purpose flour
- 2 cups milk
- 2 cups shredded sharp cheddar cheese
- 1/2 cup grated Parmesan cheese
- 1 tablespoon truffle oil
- Salt and pepper to taste
- Fresh parsley for garnish

Instructions:

1. **Cook Pasta:** Boil macaroni according to package instructions. Drain and set aside.
2. **Make Cheese Sauce:** In a saucepan, melt butter over medium heat. Stir in flour and cook for 1 minute. Gradually whisk in milk, cooking until thickened. Stir in cheddar and Parmesan until melted.
3. **Combine:** Add cooked macaroni and truffle oil to the cheese sauce. Mix well and season with salt and pepper.
4. **Serve:** Garnish with fresh parsley before serving.

Lobster Mac and Cheese

Ingredients:

- 8 oz elbow macaroni
- 2 tablespoons butter
- 2 tablespoons all-purpose flour
- 2 cups milk
- 2 cups shredded Gruyère cheese
- 1 cup cooked lobster meat, chopped
- 1/2 cup breadcrumbs
- 1 tablespoon lemon juice
- Salt and pepper to taste

Instructions:

1. **Cook Pasta:** Boil macaroni according to package instructions. Drain and set aside.
2. **Make Cheese Sauce:** In a saucepan, melt butter over medium heat. Stir in flour and cook for 1 minute. Gradually whisk in milk, cooking until thickened. Stir in Gruyère until melted.
3. **Combine:** Add lobster meat, cooked macaroni, and lemon juice to the cheese sauce. Mix well and season with salt and pepper.
4. **Bake:** Transfer to a baking dish, sprinkle breadcrumbs on top, and bake at 350°F (175°C) for 20 minutes until golden.

Buffalo Chicken Mac and Cheese

Ingredients:

- 8 oz elbow macaroni
- 2 tablespoons butter
- 2 tablespoons all-purpose flour
- 2 cups milk
- 2 cups shredded cheddar cheese
- 1 cup cooked chicken, shredded
- 1/2 cup buffalo sauce
- 1/4 cup blue cheese crumbles (optional)
- Green onions for garnish

Instructions:

1. **Cook Pasta:** Boil macaroni according to package instructions. Drain and set aside.
2. **Make Cheese Sauce:** In a saucepan, melt butter over medium heat. Stir in flour and cook for 1 minute. Gradually whisk in milk, cooking until thickened. Stir in cheddar until melted.
3. **Combine:** Add chicken and buffalo sauce to the cheese sauce. Mix well, then add cooked macaroni. Stir until combined.
4. **Serve:** Top with blue cheese and garnish with green onions.

Bacon and Cheddar Mac and Cheese

Ingredients:

- 8 oz elbow macaroni
- 4 slices bacon, chopped
- 2 tablespoons butter
- 2 tablespoons all-purpose flour
- 2 cups milk
- 2 cups shredded cheddar cheese
- Salt and pepper to taste

Instructions:

1. **Cook Pasta:** Boil macaroni according to package instructions. Drain and set aside.
2. **Cook Bacon:** In a skillet, cook bacon until crispy. Remove and drain on paper towels.
3. **Make Cheese Sauce:** In a saucepan, melt butter over medium heat. Stir in flour and cook for 1 minute. Gradually whisk in milk, cooking until thickened. Stir in cheddar until melted.
4. **Combine:** Add cooked macaroni and bacon to the cheese sauce. Mix well and season with salt and pepper.

Spinach and Artichoke Mac and Cheese

Ingredients:

- 8 oz elbow macaroni
- 2 tablespoons butter
- 2 tablespoons all-purpose flour
- 2 cups milk
- 2 cups shredded mozzarella cheese
- 1 cup canned artichoke hearts, chopped
- 1 cup fresh spinach, chopped
- 1/2 cup cream cheese
- Salt and pepper to taste

Instructions:

1. **Cook Pasta:** Boil macaroni according to package instructions. Drain and set aside.
2. **Make Cheese Sauce:** In a saucepan, melt butter over medium heat. Stir in flour and cook for 1 minute. Gradually whisk in milk, cooking until thickened. Stir in mozzarella and cream cheese until melted.
3. **Combine:** Add spinach and artichokes to the cheese sauce. Mix in cooked macaroni and season with salt and pepper.
4. **Serve:** Enjoy warm as a main dish.

Jalapeño Popper Mac and Cheese

Ingredients:

- 8 oz elbow macaroni
- 2 tablespoons butter
- 2 tablespoons all-purpose flour
- 2 cups milk
- 2 cups shredded cheddar cheese
- 1/2 cup cream cheese
- 2 jalapeños, diced (seeds removed for less heat)
- 1/4 cup breadcrumbs
- Salt and pepper to taste

Instructions:

1. **Cook Pasta:** Boil macaroni according to package instructions. Drain and set aside.
2. **Make Cheese Sauce:** In a saucepan, melt butter over medium heat. Stir in flour and cook for 1 minute. Gradually whisk in milk, cooking until thickened. Stir in cheddar and cream cheese until melted.
3. **Combine:** Add diced jalapeños and cooked macaroni to the cheese sauce. Mix well and season with salt and pepper.
4. **Bake:** Transfer to a baking dish, sprinkle breadcrumbs on top, and bake at 350°F (175°C) for 20 minutes until golden.

Mac and Cheese with Butternut Squash

Ingredients:

- 8 oz elbow macaroni
- 2 cups butternut squash, cubed
- 2 tablespoons butter
- 2 tablespoons all-purpose flour
- 2 cups milk
- 2 cups shredded cheddar cheese
- Salt and pepper to taste

Instructions:

1. **Cook Pasta:** Boil macaroni according to package instructions. Drain and set aside.
2. **Cook Squash:** Steam or boil butternut squash until tender, then mash.
3. **Make Cheese Sauce:** In a saucepan, melt butter over medium heat. Stir in flour and cook for 1 minute. Gradually whisk in milk, cooking until thickened. Stir in cheddar until melted.
4. **Combine:** Mix in mashed butternut squash and cooked macaroni. Season with salt and pepper before serving.

Pesto Mac and Cheese

Ingredients:

- 8 oz elbow macaroni
- 2 tablespoons butter
- 2 tablespoons all-purpose flour
- 2 cups milk
- 2 cups shredded mozzarella cheese
- 1/2 cup pesto
- Salt and pepper to taste

Instructions:

1. **Cook Pasta:** Boil macaroni according to package instructions. Drain and set aside.
2. **Make Cheese Sauce:** In a saucepan, melt butter over medium heat. Stir in flour and cook for 1 minute. Gradually whisk in milk, cooking until thickened. Stir in mozzarella until melted.
3. **Combine:** Add pesto and cooked macaroni to the cheese sauce. Mix well and season with salt and pepper before serving.

Mac and Cheese with Roasted Garlic

Ingredients:

- 8 oz elbow macaroni
- 1 head of garlic
- 2 tablespoons olive oil
- 2 tablespoons butter
- 2 tablespoons all-purpose flour
- 2 cups milk
- 2 cups shredded cheddar cheese
- Salt and pepper to taste
- Fresh parsley for garnish

Instructions:

1. **Roast Garlic:** Preheat oven to 400°F (200°C). Cut the top off the garlic head, drizzle with olive oil, wrap in foil, and roast for 30-35 minutes until soft. Squeeze out the garlic cloves and set aside.
2. **Cook Pasta:** Boil macaroni according to package instructions. Drain and set aside.
3. **Make Cheese Sauce:** In a saucepan, melt butter over medium heat. Stir in flour and cook for 1 minute. Gradually whisk in milk, cooking until thickened. Stir in cheese until melted, then mix in roasted garlic.
4. **Combine:** Add cooked macaroni to the cheese sauce, mixing well. Season with salt and pepper before serving, garnished with parsley.

Greek Mac and Cheese with Feta and Spinach

Ingredients:

- 8 oz elbow macaroni
- 2 tablespoons butter
- 2 tablespoons all-purpose flour
- 2 cups milk
- 2 cups shredded mozzarella cheese
- 1 cup feta cheese, crumbled
- 2 cups fresh spinach, chopped
- 1 teaspoon dried oregano
- Salt and pepper to taste

Instructions:

1. **Cook Pasta:** Boil macaroni according to package instructions. Drain and set aside.
2. **Make Cheese Sauce:** In a saucepan, melt butter over medium heat. Stir in flour and cook for 1 minute. Gradually whisk in milk, cooking until thickened. Stir in mozzarella and feta until melted.
3. **Combine:** Add spinach and cooked macaroni to the cheese sauce. Stir in oregano and season with salt and pepper before serving.

Smoked Gouda Mac and Cheese

Ingredients:

- 8 oz elbow macaroni
- 2 tablespoons butter
- 2 tablespoons all-purpose flour
- 2 cups milk
- 2 cups shredded smoked Gouda cheese
- 1/2 cup breadcrumbs
- Salt and pepper to taste

Instructions:

1. **Cook Pasta:** Boil macaroni according to package instructions. Drain and set aside.
2. **Make Cheese Sauce:** In a saucepan, melt butter over medium heat. Stir in flour and cook for 1 minute. Gradually whisk in milk, cooking until thickened. Stir in smoked Gouda until melted.
3. **Combine:** Mix cooked macaroni into the cheese sauce, seasoning with salt and pepper. Transfer to a baking dish, top with breadcrumbs, and bake at 350°F (175°C) for 20 minutes until golden.

Mac and Cheese with Caramelized Onions

Ingredients:

- 8 oz elbow macaroni
- 2 tablespoons butter
- 2 large onions, thinly sliced
- 2 tablespoons all-purpose flour
- 2 cups milk
- 2 cups shredded cheddar cheese
- Salt and pepper to taste

Instructions:

1. **Caramelize Onions:** In a skillet, melt butter over medium heat. Add onions and cook slowly until caramelized, about 20-25 minutes.
2. **Cook Pasta:** Boil macaroni according to package instructions. Drain and set aside.
3. **Make Cheese Sauce:** In a saucepan, melt butter. Stir in flour and cook for 1 minute. Gradually whisk in milk, cooking until thickened. Stir in cheddar until melted.
4. **Combine:** Add caramelized onions and cooked macaroni to the cheese sauce. Mix well and season with salt and pepper before serving.

Mac and Cheese with Brussels Sprouts

Ingredients:

- 8 oz elbow macaroni
- 2 cups Brussels sprouts, halved
- 2 tablespoons butter
- 2 tablespoons all-purpose flour
- 2 cups milk
- 2 cups shredded cheddar cheese
- Salt and pepper to taste

Instructions:

1. **Cook Brussels Sprouts:** Steam Brussels sprouts until tender, about 5-7 minutes. Set aside.
2. **Cook Pasta:** Boil macaroni according to package instructions. Drain and set aside.
3. **Make Cheese Sauce:** In a saucepan, melt butter over medium heat. Stir in flour and cook for 1 minute. Gradually whisk in milk, cooking until thickened. Stir in cheddar until melted.
4. **Combine:** Add cooked macaroni and Brussels sprouts to the cheese sauce, mixing well. Season with salt and pepper before serving.

BBQ Pulled Pork Mac and Cheese

Ingredients:

- 8 oz elbow macaroni
- 2 tablespoons butter
- 2 tablespoons all-purpose flour
- 2 cups milk
- 2 cups shredded cheddar cheese
- 1 cup pulled pork
- 1/2 cup BBQ sauce
- Salt and pepper to taste

Instructions:

1. **Cook Pasta:** Boil macaroni according to package instructions. Drain and set aside.
2. **Make Cheese Sauce:** In a saucepan, melt butter over medium heat. Stir in flour and cook for 1 minute. Gradually whisk in milk, cooking until thickened. Stir in cheddar until melted.
3. **Combine:** Add pulled pork and BBQ sauce to the cheese sauce. Mix in cooked macaroni, seasoning with salt and pepper before serving.

Mac and Cheese with Blue Cheese and Pear

Ingredients:

- 8 oz elbow macaroni
- 2 tablespoons butter
- 2 tablespoons all-purpose flour
- 2 cups milk
- 1 cup shredded cheddar cheese
- 1 cup crumbled blue cheese
- 1 ripe pear, diced
- Salt and pepper to taste

Instructions:

1. **Cook Pasta:** Boil macaroni according to package instructions. Drain and set aside.
2. **Make Cheese Sauce:** In a saucepan, melt butter over medium heat. Stir in flour and cook for 1 minute. Gradually whisk in milk, cooking until thickened. Stir in cheddar and blue cheese until melted.
3. **Combine:** Add diced pear and cooked macaroni to the cheese sauce. Mix well and season with salt and pepper before serving.

Mac and Cheese with Wild Mushrooms

Ingredients:

- 8 oz elbow macaroni
- 2 tablespoons butter
- 2 cups wild mushrooms, sliced
- 2 tablespoons all-purpose flour
- 2 cups milk
- 2 cups shredded cheddar cheese
- Salt and pepper to taste
- Fresh thyme for garnish

Instructions:

1. **Cook Pasta:** Boil macaroni according to package instructions. Drain and set aside.
2. **Sauté Mushrooms:** In a skillet, melt butter over medium heat. Add mushrooms and cook until soft, about 5-7 minutes.
3. **Make Cheese Sauce:** In a saucepan, melt butter. Stir in flour and cook for 1 minute. Gradually whisk in milk, cooking until thickened. Stir in cheddar until melted.
4. **Combine:** Add sautéed mushrooms and cooked macaroni to the cheese sauce. Mix well, season with salt and pepper, and garnish with fresh thyme before serving.

Mac and Cheese with Sriracha and Lime

Ingredients:

- 8 oz elbow macaroni
- 2 tablespoons butter
- 2 tablespoons all-purpose flour
- 2 cups milk
- 2 cups shredded cheddar cheese
- 2 tablespoons Sriracha sauce (or to taste)
- Juice of 1 lime
- Zest of 1 lime
- Salt and pepper to taste
- Chopped cilantro for garnish

Instructions:

1. **Cook Pasta:** Boil macaroni according to package instructions. Drain and set aside.
2. **Make Cheese Sauce:** In a saucepan, melt butter over medium heat. Stir in flour and cook for 1 minute. Gradually whisk in milk, cooking until thickened. Stir in cheddar until melted.
3. **Add Flavor:** Mix in Sriracha, lime juice, and lime zest. Season with salt and pepper.
4. **Combine:** Add cooked macaroni to the cheese sauce, stirring well. Garnish with cilantro before serving.

Creamy Tomato Basil Mac and Cheese

Ingredients:

- 8 oz elbow macaroni
- 1 can (14 oz) diced tomatoes, drained
- 2 tablespoons butter
- 2 tablespoons all-purpose flour
- 2 cups milk
- 2 cups shredded mozzarella cheese
- 1/2 cup grated Parmesan cheese
- 1/4 cup fresh basil, chopped
- Salt and pepper to taste

Instructions:

1. **Cook Pasta:** Boil macaroni according to package instructions. Drain and set aside.
2. **Make Cheese Sauce:** In a saucepan, melt butter over medium heat. Stir in flour and cook for 1 minute. Gradually whisk in milk, cooking until thickened. Stir in mozzarella and Parmesan until melted.
3. **Add Tomatoes and Basil:** Stir in drained tomatoes and chopped basil. Season with salt and pepper.
4. **Combine:** Add cooked macaroni to the sauce, mixing well before serving.

Baked Mac and Cheese with Herb Breadcrumbs

Ingredients:

- 8 oz elbow macaroni
- 2 tablespoons butter
- 2 tablespoons all-purpose flour
- 2 cups milk
- 2 cups shredded cheddar cheese
- 1 cup breadcrumbs
- 2 tablespoons olive oil
- 1 teaspoon dried herbs (e.g., thyme, oregano)
- Salt and pepper to taste

Instructions:

1. **Cook Pasta:** Boil macaroni according to package instructions. Drain and set aside.
2. **Make Cheese Sauce:** In a saucepan, melt butter over medium heat. Stir in flour and cook for 1 minute. Gradually whisk in milk, cooking until thickened. Stir in cheddar until melted.
3. **Prepare Breadcrumb Topping:** In a bowl, mix breadcrumbs with olive oil, herbs, and a pinch of salt.
4. **Combine and Bake:** Add cooked macaroni to the cheese sauce. Transfer to a baking dish, top with breadcrumbs, and bake at 350°F (175°C) for 20-25 minutes until golden.

Mac and Cheese with Crab and Old Bay

Ingredients:

- 8 oz elbow macaroni
- 2 tablespoons butter
- 2 tablespoons all-purpose flour
- 2 cups milk
- 2 cups shredded cheddar cheese
- 1 cup lump crab meat
- 1 tablespoon Old Bay seasoning
- Salt and pepper to taste

Instructions:

1. **Cook Pasta:** Boil macaroni according to package instructions. Drain and set aside.
2. **Make Cheese Sauce:** In a saucepan, melt butter over medium heat. Stir in flour and cook for 1 minute. Gradually whisk in milk, cooking until thickened. Stir in cheddar until melted.
3. **Add Crab and Seasoning:** Gently fold in crab meat and Old Bay seasoning. Season with salt and pepper.
4. **Combine:** Add cooked macaroni to the cheese sauce, mixing well before serving.

Mac and Cheese with Roasted Red Peppers

Ingredients:

- 8 oz elbow macaroni
- 2 tablespoons butter
- 2 tablespoons all-purpose flour
- 2 cups milk
- 2 cups shredded cheddar cheese
- 1 cup roasted red peppers, diced
- Salt and pepper to taste

Instructions:

1. **Cook Pasta:** Boil macaroni according to package instructions. Drain and set aside.
2. **Make Cheese Sauce:** In a saucepan, melt butter over medium heat. Stir in flour and cook for 1 minute. Gradually whisk in milk, cooking until thickened. Stir in cheddar until melted.
3. **Add Peppers:** Stir in roasted red peppers and season with salt and pepper.
4. **Combine:** Add cooked macaroni to the cheese sauce, mixing well before serving.

Mac and Cheese with Ground Beef and Chili

Ingredients:

- 8 oz elbow macaroni
- 1 lb ground beef
- 2 tablespoons chili powder
- 2 tablespoons butter
- 2 tablespoons all-purpose flour
- 2 cups milk
- 2 cups shredded cheddar cheese
- Salt and pepper to taste

Instructions:

1. **Cook Beef:** In a skillet, cook ground beef over medium heat until browned. Drain excess fat, then stir in chili powder. Set aside.
2. **Cook Pasta:** Boil macaroni according to package instructions. Drain and set aside.
3. **Make Cheese Sauce:** In a saucepan, melt butter over medium heat. Stir in flour and cook for 1 minute. Gradually whisk in milk, cooking until thickened. Stir in cheddar until melted.
4. **Combine:** Add cooked macaroni and seasoned beef to the cheese sauce, mixing well before serving.

Mac and Cheese with Chicken and Broccoli

Ingredients:

- 8 oz elbow macaroni
- 2 cups broccoli florets
- 2 tablespoons butter
- 2 tablespoons all-purpose flour
- 2 cups milk
- 2 cups shredded cheddar cheese
- Salt and pepper to taste

Instructions:

1. **Cook Pasta and Broccoli:** Boil macaroni according to package instructions, adding broccoli florets for the last 3-4 minutes of cooking. Drain and set aside.
2. **Make Cheese Sauce:** In a saucepan, melt butter over medium heat. Stir in flour and cook for 1 minute. Gradually whisk in milk, cooking until thickened. Stir in cheddar until melted.
3. **Combine:** Add cooked macaroni and broccoli to the cheese sauce, mixing well. Season with salt and pepper before serving.

Mac and Cheese with Spicy Italian Sausage

Ingredients:

- 8 oz elbow macaroni
- 1 lb spicy Italian sausage, casings removed
- 2 tablespoons butter
- 2 tablespoons all-purpose flour
- 2 cups milk
- 2 cups shredded mozzarella cheese
- Salt and pepper to taste

Instructions:

1. **Cook Sausage:** In a skillet, cook sausage over medium heat until browned. Drain excess fat and set aside.
2. **Cook Pasta:** Boil macaroni according to package instructions. Drain and set aside.
3. **Make Cheese Sauce:** In a saucepan, melt butter over medium heat. Stir in flour and cook for 1 minute. Gradually whisk in milk, cooking until thickened. Stir in mozzarella until melted.
4. **Combine:** Add cooked macaroni and sausage to the cheese sauce, mixing well before serving.

Mac and Cheese with Goat Cheese and Thyme

Ingredients:

- 8 oz elbow macaroni
- 2 tablespoons butter
- 2 tablespoons all-purpose flour
- 2 cups milk
- 1 cup goat cheese, crumbled
- 1 teaspoon fresh thyme leaves
- Salt and pepper to taste
- Grated Parmesan cheese for topping

Instructions:

1. **Cook Pasta:** Boil macaroni according to package instructions. Drain and set aside.
2. **Make Cheese Sauce:** In a saucepan, melt butter over medium heat. Stir in flour and cook for 1 minute. Gradually whisk in milk, cooking until thickened. Stir in goat cheese and thyme until melted and smooth.
3. **Combine:** Add cooked macaroni to the cheese sauce, mixing well. Transfer to a baking dish, sprinkle with Parmesan, and broil until golden.

Mac and Cheese with Pumpkin and Sage

Ingredients:

- 8 oz elbow macaroni
- 2 tablespoons butter
- 2 tablespoons all-purpose flour
- 2 cups milk
- 1 cup pumpkin puree
- 1 teaspoon dried sage
- 2 cups shredded cheddar cheese
- Salt and pepper to taste

Instructions:

1. **Cook Pasta:** Boil macaroni according to package instructions. Drain and set aside.
2. **Make Cheese Sauce:** In a saucepan, melt butter over medium heat. Stir in flour and cook for 1 minute. Gradually whisk in milk, then add pumpkin and sage, stirring until combined. Stir in cheddar until melted.
3. **Combine:** Add cooked macaroni to the sauce, mixing well before serving.

Mac and Cheese with Cauliflower and Cheese Sauce

Ingredients:

- 8 oz elbow macaroni
- 2 cups cauliflower florets
- 2 tablespoons butter
- 2 tablespoons all-purpose flour
- 2 cups milk
- 2 cups shredded cheddar cheese
- Salt and pepper to taste

Instructions:

1. **Cook Pasta and Cauliflower:** Boil macaroni according to package instructions, adding cauliflower florets for the last 3-4 minutes of cooking. Drain and set aside.
2. **Make Cheese Sauce:** In a saucepan, melt butter over medium heat. Stir in flour and cook for 1 minute. Gradually whisk in milk, cooking until thickened. Stir in cheddar until melted.
3. **Combine:** Add cooked macaroni and cauliflower to the cheese sauce, mixing well before serving.

Mac and Cheese with Roasted Eggplant

Ingredients:

- 8 oz elbow macaroni
- 1 medium eggplant, diced and roasted
- 2 tablespoons butter
- 2 tablespoons all-purpose flour
- 2 cups milk
- 2 cups shredded mozzarella cheese
- Salt and pepper to taste

Instructions:

1. **Cook Pasta:** Boil macaroni according to package instructions. Drain and set aside.
2. **Roast Eggplant:** Toss diced eggplant with olive oil, salt, and pepper; roast at 400°F (200°C) for 20-25 minutes until tender.
3. **Make Cheese Sauce:** In a saucepan, melt butter over medium heat. Stir in flour and cook for 1 minute. Gradually whisk in milk, cooking until thickened. Stir in mozzarella until melted.
4. **Combine:** Add cooked macaroni and roasted eggplant to the cheese sauce, mixing well before serving.

Mac and Cheese with Zucchini and Herbs

Ingredients:

- 8 oz elbow macaroni
- 2 cups zucchini, diced
- 2 tablespoons butter
- 2 tablespoons all-purpose flour
- 2 cups milk
- 2 cups shredded cheddar cheese
- 1 tablespoon fresh herbs (e.g., basil, parsley)
- Salt and pepper to taste

Instructions:

1. **Cook Pasta and Zucchini:** Boil macaroni according to package instructions. Add zucchini for the last 3-4 minutes. Drain and set aside.
2. **Make Cheese Sauce:** In a saucepan, melt butter over medium heat. Stir in flour and cook for 1 minute. Gradually whisk in milk, cooking until thickened. Stir in cheddar until melted and mix in herbs.
3. **Combine:** Add cooked macaroni and zucchini to the sauce, mixing well before serving.

Mac and Cheese with Boursin and Spinach

Ingredients:

- 8 oz elbow macaroni
- 2 cups fresh spinach
- 2 tablespoons butter
- 2 tablespoons all-purpose flour
- 2 cups milk
- 1 cup Boursin cheese
- Salt and pepper to taste

Instructions:

1. **Cook Pasta:** Boil macaroni according to package instructions. Drain and set aside.
2. **Sauté Spinach:** In a skillet, melt butter and sauté spinach until wilted. Set aside.
3. **Make Cheese Sauce:** In a saucepan, melt butter over medium heat. Stir in flour and cook for 1 minute. Gradually whisk in milk, cooking until thickened. Stir in Boursin until melted.
4. **Combine:** Add cooked macaroni and sautéed spinach to the sauce, mixing well before serving.

Mac and Cheese with Smoked Salmon

Ingredients:

- 8 oz elbow macaroni
- 4 oz smoked salmon, chopped
- 2 tablespoons butter
- 2 tablespoons all-purpose flour
- 2 cups milk
- 2 cups shredded mozzarella cheese
- 1 tablespoon capers (optional)
- Salt and pepper to taste

Instructions:

1. **Cook Pasta:** Boil macaroni according to package instructions. Drain and set aside.
2. **Make Cheese Sauce:** In a saucepan, melt butter over medium heat. Stir in flour and cook for 1 minute. Gradually whisk in milk, cooking until thickened. Stir in mozzarella until melted.
3. **Combine:** Add cooked macaroni, smoked salmon, and capers (if using) to the sauce, mixing well before serving.

Mac and Cheese with Sweet Potatoes and Pecans

Ingredients:

- 8 oz elbow macaroni
- 1 cup sweet potatoes, peeled and diced
- 2 tablespoons butter
- 2 tablespoons all-purpose flour
- 2 cups milk
- 2 cups shredded cheddar cheese
- 1/2 cup pecans, toasted
- Salt and pepper to taste

Instructions:

1. **Cook Pasta and Sweet Potatoes:** Boil macaroni according to package instructions. For the last 5 minutes, add diced sweet potatoes. Drain and set aside.
2. **Make Cheese Sauce:** In a saucepan, melt butter over medium heat. Stir in flour and cook for 1 minute. Gradually whisk in milk, cooking until thickened. Stir in cheddar until melted.
3. **Combine:** Add cooked macaroni and sweet potatoes to the cheese sauce. Stir in toasted pecans and season with salt and pepper before serving.

Mac and Cheese with Chorizo and Corn

Ingredients:

- 8 oz elbow macaroni
- 1 cup chorizo, diced
- 1 cup corn kernels (fresh, frozen, or canned)
- 2 tablespoons butter
- 2 tablespoons all-purpose flour
- 2 cups milk
- 2 cups shredded cheddar cheese
- Salt and pepper to taste

Instructions:

1. **Cook Pasta:** Boil macaroni according to package instructions. Drain and set aside.
2. **Cook Chorizo:** In a skillet, cook chorizo over medium heat until browned. Add corn and cook for an additional 2-3 minutes. Set aside.
3. **Make Cheese Sauce:** In a saucepan, melt butter over medium heat. Stir in flour and cook for 1 minute. Gradually whisk in milk, cooking until thickened. Stir in cheddar until melted.
4. **Combine:** Add cooked macaroni, chorizo, and corn to the cheese sauce, mixing well before serving.

Mac and Cheese with Pimento Cheese

Ingredients:

- 8 oz elbow macaroni
- 1 cup pimento cheese spread
- 2 tablespoons butter
- 2 tablespoons all-purpose flour
- 2 cups milk
- 1 cup shredded cheddar cheese (optional)
- Salt and pepper to taste

Instructions:

1. **Cook Pasta:** Boil macaroni according to package instructions. Drain and set aside.
2. **Make Cheese Sauce:** In a saucepan, melt butter over medium heat. Stir in flour and cook for 1 minute. Gradually whisk in milk, cooking until thickened. Stir in pimento cheese until melted.
3. **Combine:** If desired, mix in cheddar cheese, then add cooked macaroni to the sauce, mixing well before serving.

Mac and Cheese with Peas and Prosciutto

Ingredients:

- 8 oz elbow macaroni
- 1 cup frozen peas
- 4 oz prosciutto, diced
- 2 tablespoons butter
- 2 tablespoons all-purpose flour
- 2 cups milk
- 2 cups shredded mozzarella cheese
- Salt and pepper to taste

Instructions:

1. **Cook Pasta:** Boil macaroni according to package instructions, adding peas for the last 2-3 minutes. Drain and set aside.
2. **Cook Prosciutto:** In a skillet, cook prosciutto over medium heat until crispy. Set aside.
3. **Make Cheese Sauce:** In a saucepan, melt butter over medium heat. Stir in flour and cook for 1 minute. Gradually whisk in milk, cooking until thickened. Stir in mozzarella until melted.
4. **Combine:** Add cooked macaroni, peas, and prosciutto to the cheese sauce, mixing well before serving.

Mac and Cheese with Artichokes and Parmesan

Ingredients:

- 8 oz elbow macaroni
- 1 can (14 oz) artichoke hearts, drained and chopped
- 2 tablespoons butter
- 2 tablespoons all-purpose flour
- 2 cups milk
- 1 cup grated Parmesan cheese
- 1 teaspoon garlic powder
- Salt and pepper to taste

Instructions:

1. **Cook Pasta:** Boil macaroni according to package instructions. Drain and set aside.
2. **Make Cheese Sauce:** In a saucepan, melt butter over medium heat. Stir in flour and cook for 1 minute. Gradually whisk in milk, cooking until thickened. Stir in Parmesan and garlic powder until melted.
3. **Combine:** Add cooked macaroni and artichokes to the cheese sauce, mixing well before serving.

Mac and Cheese with Bacon and Egg

Ingredients:

- 8 oz elbow macaroni
- 4 strips of bacon, cooked and crumbled
- 2 large eggs
- 2 tablespoons butter
- 2 tablespoons all-purpose flour
- 2 cups milk
- 2 cups shredded cheddar cheese
- Salt and pepper to taste

Instructions:

1. **Cook Pasta:** Boil macaroni according to package instructions. Drain and set aside.
2. **Cook Bacon:** In a skillet, cook bacon until crispy. Set aside and reserve some bacon fat.
3. **Make Cheese Sauce:** In a saucepan, melt butter (or bacon fat) over medium heat. Stir in flour and cook for 1 minute. Gradually whisk in milk, cooking until thickened. Stir in cheddar until melted.
4. **Combine:** In a bowl, beat eggs. Mix cooked macaroni, crumbled bacon, and cheese sauce. Add beaten eggs and mix well before serving.

Mac and Cheese with Truffle Oil and Parmesan

Ingredients:

- 8 oz elbow macaroni
- 2 tablespoons truffle oil
- 2 tablespoons butter
- 2 tablespoons all-purpose flour
- 2 cups milk
- 1 cup grated Parmesan cheese
- Salt and pepper to taste

Instructions:

1. **Cook Pasta:** Boil macaroni according to package instructions. Drain and set aside.
2. **Make Cheese Sauce:** In a saucepan, melt butter over medium heat. Stir in flour and cook for 1 minute. Gradually whisk in milk, cooking until thickened. Stir in Parmesan until melted.
3. **Combine:** Add cooked macaroni and truffle oil to the cheese sauce, mixing well before serving.

Mac and Cheese with Cilantro and Lime

Ingredients:

- 8 oz elbow macaroni
- 1/4 cup fresh cilantro, chopped
- 1 tablespoon lime juice
- 2 tablespoons butter
- 2 tablespoons all-purpose flour
- 2 cups milk
- 2 cups shredded cheddar cheese
- Salt and pepper to taste

Instructions:

1. **Cook Pasta:** Boil macaroni according to package instructions. Drain and set aside.
2. **Make Cheese Sauce:** In a saucepan, melt butter over medium heat. Stir in flour and cook for 1 minute. Gradually whisk in milk, cooking until thickened. Stir in cheddar until melted.
3. **Combine:** Add cooked macaroni, cilantro, and lime juice to the cheese sauce, mixing well before serving.

Mac and Cheese with Roasted Veggies

Ingredients:

- 8 oz elbow macaroni
- 2 cups mixed vegetables (e.g., bell peppers, zucchini, broccoli), roasted
- 2 tablespoons butter
- 2 tablespoons all-purpose flour
- 2 cups milk
- 2 cups shredded cheddar cheese
- Salt and pepper to taste

Instructions:

1. **Cook Pasta:** Boil macaroni according to package instructions. Drain and set aside.
2. **Roast Vegetables:** Toss mixed vegetables with olive oil, salt, and pepper, and roast at 400°F (200°C) for 20-25 minutes.
3. **Make Cheese Sauce:** In a saucepan, melt butter over medium heat. Stir in flour and cook for 1 minute. Gradually whisk in milk, cooking until thickened. Stir in cheddar until melted.
4. **Combine:** Add cooked macaroni and roasted veggies to the cheese sauce, mixing well before serving.

Mac and Cheese with Italian Herbs and Cheese

Ingredients:

- 8 oz elbow macaroni
- 2 tablespoons butter
- 2 tablespoons all-purpose flour
- 2 cups milk
- 2 cups shredded mozzarella cheese
- 1 cup grated Parmesan cheese
- 1 teaspoon Italian seasoning
- Salt and pepper to taste

Instructions:

1. **Cook Pasta:** Boil macaroni according to package instructions. Drain and set aside.
2. **Make Cheese Sauce:** In a saucepan, melt butter over medium heat. Stir in flour and cook for 1 minute. Gradually whisk in milk, cooking until thickened. Stir in mozzarella, Parmesan, and Italian seasoning until melted.
3. **Combine:** Add cooked macaroni to the cheese sauce, mixing well before serving.

Mac and Cheese with Curry and Coconut Milk

Ingredients:

- 8 oz elbow macaroni
- 1 can (14 oz) coconut milk
- 2 tablespoons curry powder
- 2 tablespoons butter
- 2 tablespoons all-purpose flour
- 1 cup shredded cheddar cheese
- Salt and pepper to taste

Instructions:

1. **Cook Pasta:** Boil macaroni according to package instructions. Drain and set aside.
2. **Make Cheese Sauce:** In a saucepan, melt butter over medium heat. Stir in flour and curry powder, cooking for 1 minute. Gradually whisk in coconut milk, cooking until thickened. Stir in cheddar until melted.
3. **Combine:** Add cooked macaroni to the sauce, mixing well before serving.

Mac and Cheese with Aged Cheddar and Mustard

Ingredients:

- 8 oz elbow macaroni
- 2 tablespoons butter
- 2 tablespoons all-purpose flour
- 2 cups milk
- 2 cups aged cheddar cheese, shredded
- 2 tablespoons Dijon mustard
- Salt and pepper to taste

Instructions:

1. **Cook Pasta:** Boil macaroni according to package instructions. Drain and set aside.
2. **Make Cheese Sauce:** In a saucepan, melt butter over medium heat. Stir in flour and cook for 1 minute. Gradually whisk in milk, cooking until thickened. Stir in aged cheddar and mustard until melted.
3. **Combine:** Add cooked macaroni to the sauce, mixing well before serving.

Mac and Cheese with Broccoli Rabe and Sausage

Ingredients:

- 8 oz elbow macaroni
- 1 cup broccoli rabe, chopped
- 4 oz Italian sausage, cooked and crumbled
- 2 tablespoons butter
- 2 tablespoons all-purpose flour
- 2 cups milk
- 2 cups shredded mozzarella cheese
- Salt and pepper to taste

Instructions:

1. **Cook Pasta:** Boil macaroni according to package instructions, adding broccoli rabe for the last 2-3 minutes. Drain and set aside.
2. **Cook Sausage:** In a skillet, cook sausage until browned. Set aside.
3. **Make Cheese Sauce:** In a saucepan, melt butter over medium heat. Stir in flour and cook for 1 minute. Gradually whisk in milk, cooking until thickened. Stir in mozzarella until melted.
4. **Combine:** Add cooked macaroni, broccoli rabe, and sausage to the cheese sauce, mixing well before serving.

Mac and Cheese with Fig and Prosciutto

Ingredients:

- 8 oz elbow macaroni
- 1 cup figs, chopped
- 4 oz prosciutto, chopped
- 2 tablespoons butter
- 2 tablespoons all-purpose flour
- 2 cups milk
- 2 cups shredded fontina cheese
- Salt and pepper to taste

Instructions:

1. **Cook Pasta:** Boil macaroni according to package instructions. Drain and set aside.
2. **Cook Prosciutto:** In a skillet, cook prosciutto until crispy. Set aside.
3. **Make Cheese Sauce:** In a saucepan, melt butter over medium heat. Stir in flour and cook for 1 minute. Gradually whisk in milk, cooking until thickened. Stir in fontina until melted.
4. **Combine:** Add cooked macaroni, figs, and prosciutto to the cheese sauce, mixing well before serving.

Mac and Cheese with Peppers and Onions

Ingredients:

- 8 oz elbow macaroni
- 1 cup bell peppers, chopped
- 1/2 cup onion, chopped
- 2 tablespoons butter
- 2 tablespoons all-purpose flour
- 2 cups milk
- 2 cups shredded cheddar cheese
- Salt and pepper to taste

Instructions:

1. **Cook Pasta:** Boil macaroni according to package instructions. Drain and set aside.
2. **Sauté Vegetables:** In a skillet, melt butter over medium heat. Add peppers and onions, cooking until softened. Set aside.
3. **Make Cheese Sauce:** In a saucepan, melt butter over medium heat. Stir in flour and cook for 1 minute. Gradually whisk in milk, cooking until thickened. Stir in cheddar until melted.
4. **Combine:** Add cooked macaroni, sautéed vegetables, and cheese sauce, mixing well before serving.

Mac and Cheese with Chicken Alfredo

Ingredients:

- 8 oz elbow macaroni
- 2 cups cooked chicken, shredded
- 2 tablespoons butter
- 2 tablespoons all-purpose flour
- 2 cups milk
- 1 cup heavy cream
- 2 cups shredded parmesan cheese
- Salt and pepper to taste

Instructions:

1. **Cook Pasta:** Boil macaroni according to package instructions. Drain and set aside.
2. **Make Alfredo Sauce:** In a saucepan, melt butter over medium heat. Stir in flour and cook for 1 minute. Gradually whisk in milk and heavy cream, cooking until thickened. Stir in Parmesan until melted.
3. **Combine:** Add cooked macaroni and chicken to the Alfredo sauce, mixing well before serving.

Mac and Cheese with Pesto and Sundried Tomatoes

Ingredients:

- 8 oz elbow macaroni
- 1/2 cup pesto
- 1/2 cup sundried tomatoes, chopped
- 2 tablespoons butter
- 2 tablespoons all-purpose flour
- 2 cups milk
- 2 cups shredded mozzarella cheese
- Salt and pepper to taste

Instructions:

1. **Cook Pasta:** Boil macaroni according to package instructions. Drain and set aside.
2. **Make Cheese Sauce:** In a saucepan, melt butter over medium heat. Stir in flour and cook for 1 minute. Gradually whisk in milk, cooking until thickened. Stir in mozzarella and pesto until melted.
3. **Combine:** Add cooked macaroni and sundried tomatoes to the cheese sauce, mixing well before serving.

Mac and Cheese with Fontina and Truffle Salt

Ingredients:

- 8 oz elbow macaroni
- 2 tablespoons butter
- 2 tablespoons all-purpose flour
- 2 cups milk
- 2 cups shredded fontina cheese
- 1 teaspoon truffle salt (or to taste)
- Freshly ground black pepper to taste
- Optional: Fresh parsley or chives for garnish

Instructions:

1. **Cook Pasta:** Boil macaroni according to package instructions. Drain and set aside.
2. **Make Cheese Sauce:** In a saucepan, melt butter over medium heat. Stir in flour and cook for 1 minute to form a roux. Gradually whisk in milk, cooking until thickened. Stir in fontina cheese until melted and smooth. Season with truffle salt and black pepper.
3. **Combine:** Add the cooked macaroni to the cheese sauce, mixing well. Adjust seasoning if needed.
4. **Serve:** Garnish with fresh parsley or chives if desired, and enjoy!

Mac and Cheese with a Mexican Twist (Chiles and Queso)

Ingredients:

- 8 oz elbow macaroni
- 1 can (4 oz) diced green chiles, drained
- 1 cup queso blanco (or cheese of choice, such as Monterey Jack)
- 1 cup shredded cheddar cheese
- 2 tablespoons butter
- 2 tablespoons all-purpose flour
- 2 cups milk
- 1 teaspoon cumin
- 1/2 teaspoon chili powder
- Salt and pepper to taste
- Optional: Fresh cilantro for garnish

Instructions:

1. **Cook Pasta:** Boil macaroni according to package instructions. Drain and set aside.
2. **Make Cheese Sauce:** In a saucepan, melt butter over medium heat. Stir in flour and cook for 1 minute. Gradually whisk in milk, cooking until thickened. Stir in queso blanco, cheddar, diced green chiles, cumin, chili powder, salt, and pepper until melted and smooth.
3. **Combine:** Add the cooked macaroni to the cheese sauce, mixing well.
4. **Serve:** Garnish with fresh cilantro if desired, and enjoy!

www.ingramcontent.com/pod-product-compliance
Lightning Source LLC
LaVergne TN
LVHW081336060526
838201LV00055B/2683